P9-BYJ-771

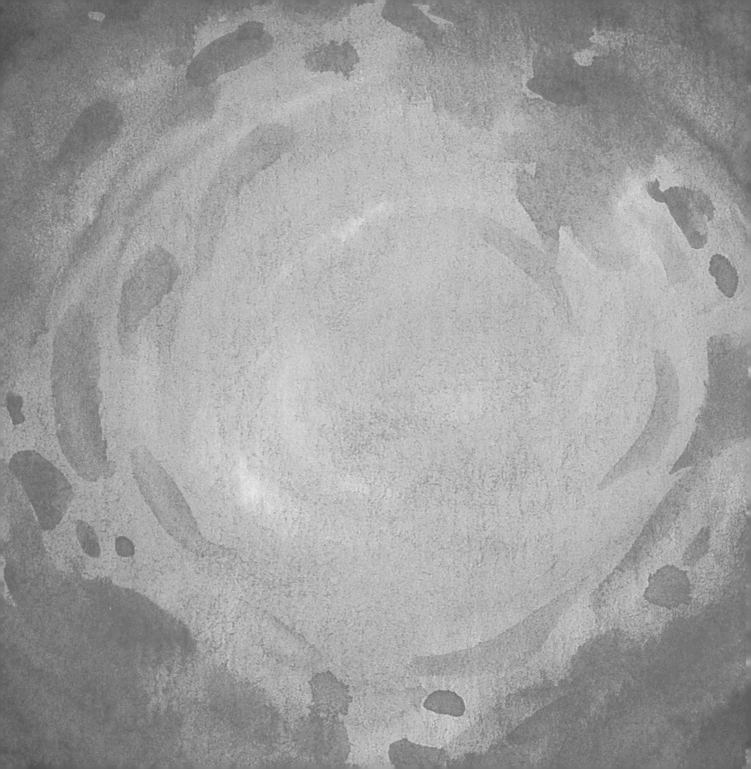

I AM HUMAN

A BOOK of EMPATHY

BY SUSAN VERDE · ART BY PETER H. REYNOLDS

Abrams Books for Young Readers · New York

To Diana G. for her creative soul
and inspiration shared over dinner.
And to my fellow humans… keep learning,
forgiving, and loving one another. —S.V.

To two great humans —Marlo Thomas & Phil Donahue. —P.H.R.

The illustrations in this book were created using ink, gouache, watercolor, and tea.

Library of Congress Cataloging-in-Publication Data
Names: Verde, Susan, author. | Reynolds, Peter H. (Peter Hamilton), 1961– illustrator.
Title: I am human: a book of empathy / by Susan Verde; illustrated by Peter H. Reynolds.
Description: New York: Abrams Books for Young Readers, 2018. | Summary: A child recognizes
his own humanity, his capacity for doing harm and being harmed, his ability to feel
joy and sadness, and his belief in hope and promise to keep learning.
Identifiers: LCCN 2017054251 | ISBN 978-1-4197-3165-5 (hardcover with jacket)
Subjects: | CYAC: Empathy—Fiction. | Compassion—Fiction. | Conduct of life—Fiction.
Classification: LCC PZ7.1.V46 Iaae 2018 | DDC [E]—dc23

Text copyright © 2018 Susan Verde
Illustrations copyright © 2018 Peter H. Reynolds
Book design by Chad W. Beckerman

Published in 2018 by Abrams Books for Young Readers, an imprint of ABRAMS. All rights
reserved. No portion of this book may be reproduced, stored in a retrieval system, or
transmitted in any form or by any means, mechanical, electronic, photocopying, recording, or
otherwise, without written permission from the publisher.
Abrams® is a registered trademark of Harry N. Abrams, Inc.

Printed and bound in U.S.A.
12 11 10 9 8 7 6

ABRAMS The Art of Books
195 Broadway, New York, NY 10007
abramsbooks.com

I was born. A miracle!
One of billions
but unique!

I am Human.

I am always learning.

I have a feeling of wonder.

I am amazed by nature.

I have a playful side.

I find joy in friendships.

I am Human.

But being human means
I am *not* perfect.
I make mistakes.

I can hurt others
with my words, my actions,
and even my silence.

I can be hurt, too.

and timid to try something new.

I have a heavy heart
when I feel sadness.

I am Human.

But then I remind myself that because I AM human, I can make choices.

I can move forward.

A poor choice
can become

a BETTER choice
with thoughtfulness.

A bad day
can become
a GREAT day
with kindness.

I can act
with compassion
and lend a helping hand.

I can treat others
with equality
and be fair.

I can choose not to fight
but instead to listen
and find common ground.

I can say,
"I'm sorry,"
and ask for forgiveness.

I am Human.

One of billions
but unique.

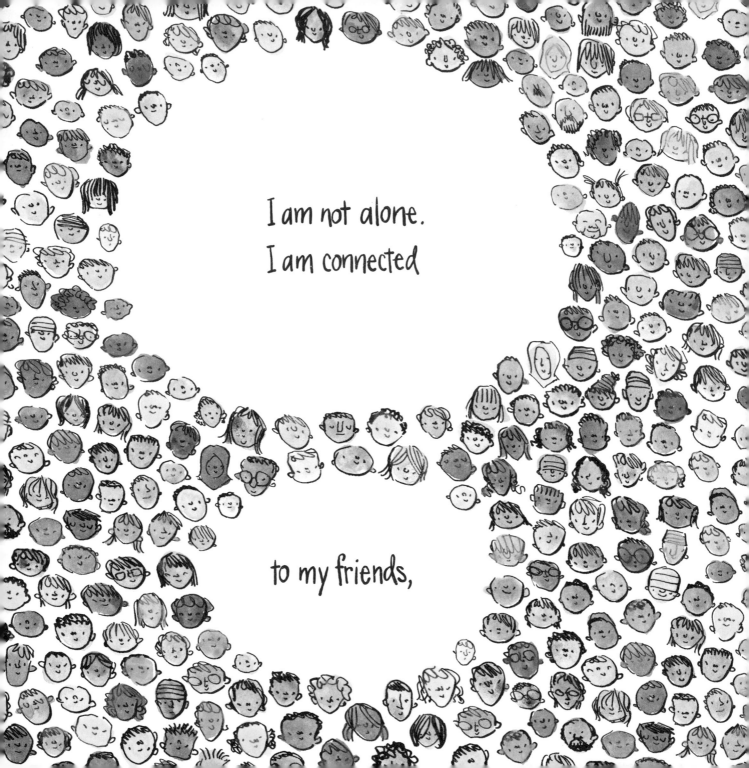

I am not alone.
I am connected

to my friends,

to my family,

to the world.

We are
all humans
together.

And I will keep
trying to be
the best version
of ME.

I am full of hope.
I am Human.

Author's Note

The journey of being human is one full of challenges. But it is also a journey full of possibilities! *I Am Human* is the story of what it means to be a human being as both an individual and within our worldwide human community. As humans, we make mistakes, but that also means we have the ability to *choose* how we respond to our mistakes. We can learn from them and change. We can be kind to one another even when it is difficult. We can choose love and compassion and celebrate the "human-ness" in all of us.

One wonderful way to share love and kindness with all humans is to practice a loving-kindness meditation. Studies have found that this practice has many positive psychological and physiological benefits. Just a few of those benefits are relaxation; a strengthening of the areas in the brain that are responsible for empathy, emotional regulation, and resilience; an increase in positive emotions and compassion; and a decrease in bias and self-criticism. Below is an example of a simple and effective loving-kindness meditation.

You will repeat these four phrases:

May you be healthy.
May you be happy.
May you be free from suffering.
May you be filled with peace.

Begin by sitting comfortably with your eyes closed. Breathe in and out slowly through your nose, and notice your breath fill your body. Imagine someone you love sitting in front of you. In your mind, tell that person the phrases above, pausing between each phrase. As you continue to breathe, feel your kind words and energy filling your heart space.

Next, imagine someone you might have challenges with, like a sibling or classmate, sitting in front of you. If that is difficult, you can choose a more neutral person. Repeat the phrases to that person and send him or her your loving energy.

Now, bring to mind the other humans on this planet who might need love, compassion, kindness, and help. Repeat your phrases and imagine sending out your loving energy with each breath.

Finally, think of yourself. Fill your own heart space with love for yourself as you repeat:

May I be healthy.
May I be happy.
May I be free from suffering.
May I be filled with peace.

Take a moment to notice how this practice makes you feel and how it affects you and your relationships over time. We have the power to learn, to grow, and to love. We are filled with possibility. We are human.